D1232924

VICTORIA & ALBERT MUSEUM

VICTORIAN AND EDWARDIAN DECORATIVE ARTS

LONDON
HER MAJESTY'S STATIONERY OFFICE

NOTE

This picture-book was issued in conjunction with the Exhibition of Victorian and Edwardian Decorative Arts held in 1952 to commemorate the centenary of the foundation of the 'Museum of Ornamental Art', the original ancestor of the Victoria and Albert Museum.

All the objects illustrated survive, and were newly photographed for the purpose of this publication.

INTRODUCTION

AFTER having been out of fashion for the past forty years, Victorian furniture and furnishings are now receiving the attention of the initiated. This new-found interest is mainly directed to those quaint and bizarre examples which seem by exaggeration to epitomize what we think of as 'Victorianism'. This picture-book, however, is not concerned with the outlandish and the retrospectively picturesque, nor, to any extent, with the routine everyday productions of the period. It concentrates instead on the work of those original designers who sought to determine the taste of the Victorian and Edwardian age. The objects depicted must not, therefore, be regarded as mere curiosities, nor as typical specimens of the period. All were in advance of popular taste, many were the result of a conscious revolt against it, and all can claim some solid merit as the work of serious designers.

It would be wrong to regard these pioneers as working in entire isolation from public demand, or as exercising no influence on the standards of mass-production. The widespread and revolutionary influence of A. W. N. Pugin and William Morris has long been generally recognized, but it can equally be claimed that the aspect of every home in the land has ultimately been affected not by them only, but also by the conventionalized arabesques of Owen Jones, the Anglo-Japanese taste represented here by Bruce Talbert's wallpaper and E. W. Godwin's table, the sophisticated naïveté of Voysey's birds, and even the 'Art Nouveau' extravagances of Charles Rennie Mackintosh. Each of these designers lived to see their highly personal —and originally derided—style become the basis for a popular fashion, so that even today there is hardly a tea-room or cinema in the country in which the furnishings do not owe something to them.

The illustrations cannot pretend to include the work of every remarkable Victorian and Edwardian designer. In several important categories it has not been possible to trace any surviving examples: thus the carpets and jewellery of Sir Matthew Digby Wyatt, who was the first Slade Professor at Cambridge, the furniture of C. L. Eastlake and Norman Shaw, and the early rugs of Sir Frank Brangwyn, R.A., have had to be omitted. Other original designers such as J. D. Sedding, G. F. Bodley, Selwyn Image, and W. R. Lethaby have had to be left out for lack of space, and for the same reason it has not been practicable to illustrate A. W. N. Pugin's metalwork, or Bruce Talbert's furniture.

One or two of the objects illustrated may be ugly, but many are certainly beautiful, and all can undoubtedly claim the right to be remembered and preserved as sincere and original expressions of the astonishing variety and vitality that characterized the seventy-three years which they cover.   P.F.

1 Group of 'Summerly's Art Manufactures' about 1847

2 Early Victorian pottery

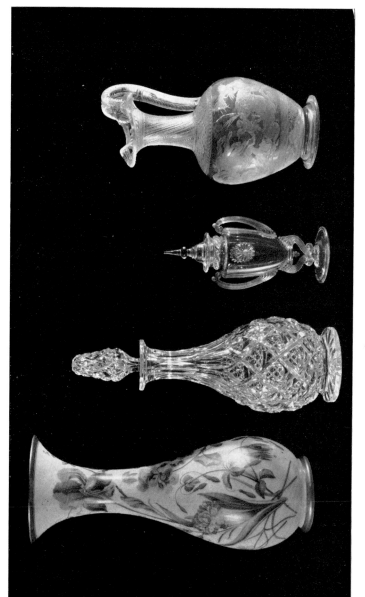

3 Early Victorian glass

4 Cabinet designed by A. W. N. Pugin, 1851

5 Stove designed by Alfred Stevens about 1852

6 Silk tissue designed by Owen Jones about 1870

7 Wallpaper frieze designed by Bruce J. Talbert, 1877

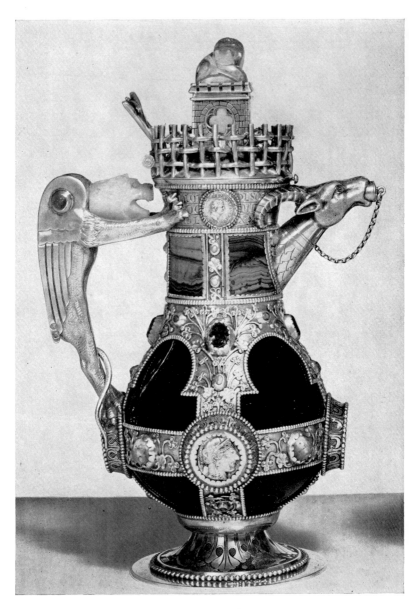

8 Decanter designed by William Burges, 1866

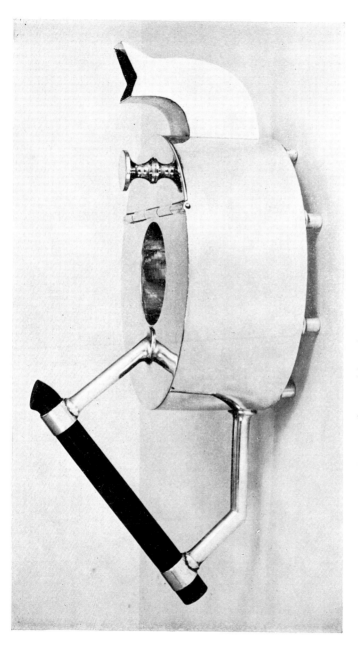

9 Teapot designed by Christopher Dresser about 1880

10 Table designed by Phillip Webb about 1870

11 Wardrobe probably designed by Philip Webb, and painted by Sir E. Burne-Jones, 1858

12 Wallpaper designed by William Morris, 1876

13 Printed cotton designed by William Morris about 1873

I am the handmaid of the earth · I broider fair her glorious gown
and deck her on her days of mirth · with many a garland of renown

and while earth's little-ones are fain · and play about the mother's hem
I scatter every gift I gain · from sun and wind to gladden them ··

14 Tapestry panel 'Flora' designed by Sir E. Burne-Jones
and William Morris, 1885

15 Pottery designed by William De Morgan, 1882–98

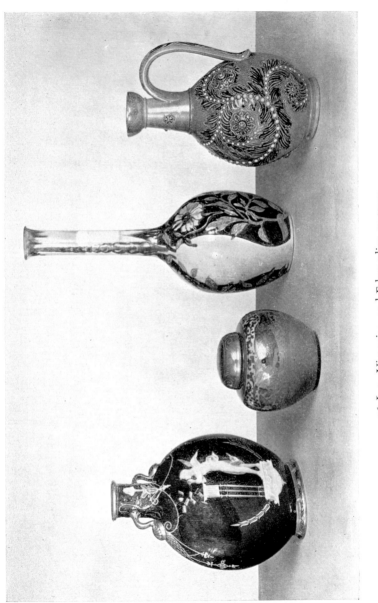

16 Late Victorian and Edwardian pottery

17 Pottery designed and made by the Martin Brothers, 1874–1903

18 Furniture designed by E. W. Godwin, 1880 and 1867

19 Printed cotton designed by A. H. Mackmurdo about 1884

20 Nursery wallpaper designed by Walter Crane, 1875

21 Machine-printed cotton designed by Lewis F. Day, 1898

22 Woven fabric designed by C. F. A. Voysey, 1899

23 Desk, chair and carpet designed by C. F. A. Voysey about 1896

24 Furniture designed by Charles Rennie Mackintosh, 1897

25 (*above*) Cushion cover designed by Jessie Newbery about 1900
(*below*) Mirror frame designed by Margaret and Frances Macdonald, 1896

26 Hall table and candlestick designed by George Walton, 1908 and 1888

27 Embroidered curtain and child's chair designed by M. H. Baillie-Scott, 1901

28 Late Victorian and Edwardian glass

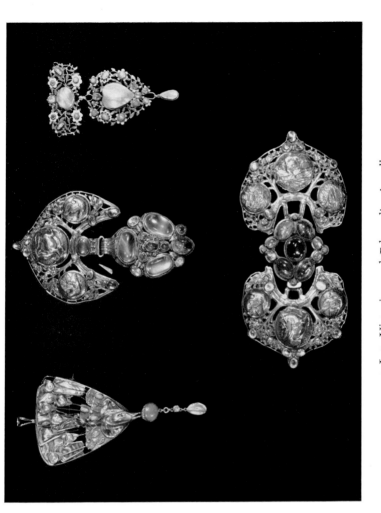

29 Late Victorian and Edwardian jewellery

30 (*above*) Teapot designed by W. A. S. Benson about 1900
(*below*) Chafing dish designed by Henry Wilson about 1906

31 Child's chair designed by Ambrose Heal, 1901

32 Cabinet designed by Ernest Gimson about 1910

NOTES

1. Group of 'Summerly's Art Manufactures' about 1847.

Wine tray, papier mâché inlaid with gold, mother-of-pearl and ivory. Designed by Richard Redgrave (1804–88) and made by Jennens and Bettridge. L. 2 ft 4¼ in. W. 1 ft. 2½ in.   32–1865

Teapot, white glazed earthenware. Part of a service designed by 'Felix Summerly' (Henry Cole) (1802–82) for the Society of Arts Competition, 1846. Made by Minton & Co. H. 6 in. W. 5½ in.   2741–1901

The 'Flax' paper-knife, gilt metal and carved ivory. The handle designed by John Bell (1811–95), the blade made and fitted by Joseph Rodgers and Sons, Sheffield. L. 10½ in. W. 1 in.   447–1865

Water carafe, glass enamelled and gilt. Designed by Richard Redgrave. H. 10¼ in. W. 5¼ in.   4503–1901

Christening cup, silver embossed and chased. Designed by Richard Redgrave and made by Harry Emanuel. H. 4⅝ in. W. 2⅝ in.   371–1865

2. Early Victorian Pottery.

Plate, painted in the 'Limoges' style by Thomas Bott at the Worcester Royal Porcelain Co.; 1867. Diam. 10⅜ in. In the possession of the makers.

Dish, painted by Emile Lessore at Wedgwoods; 1861. Diam. 15 in.
542–1894

Covered vase, made by Copelands; 1862. H. 10½ in. L. 17¾ in. W. 8¾ in.
8023–1862

Vase, designed by Alfred Stevens (1817–75) for Mintons; 1864. H. 16¾ in. Diam. 18⅞ in.   184–1864

3. Early Victorian Glass.

Vase. Painted by Thomas Bott at Richardsons, Stourbridge; about 1851. H. 17¾ in. Diam. 6⅝ in. In the possession of Benjamin Richardson, Esq.

Decanter with cut decoration. Made by Richardsons, Stourbridge; about 1851. H. 14¾ in. Diam. 5 in. In the possession of Mrs. E. Worrall.

Covered vase. Made by Isaac Barnes, Birmingham; about 1870. H. 9½ in. Diam. 2⅞ in. Given by the makers to the Birmingham City Museum and Art Gallery.

Jug, with engraved decoration. Made by James Green, London. Bought at the Great Exhibition, 1851. H. 13¼ in. Diam. 6¼ in.   4453–1901

4. Cabinet of carved and painted oak with wrought brass panels and fittings. Designed by A. W. N. Pugin (1812–52) and made by J. G. Crace. Exhibited at the Great Exhibition, 1851. H. 8 ft. W. 10 ft. D. 2 ft.   25–1852

5. Stove of cast bronze and brass, with panels of glazed earthenware. Designed by Alfred Stevens. Made by H. E. Hoole and Co., Sheffield, about 1852. H. 4 ft. 2 in. W. 2 ft. 4 in. D. 3 ft.   4030–1852

6. Silk tissue. Designed by Owen Jones (1809–74), and made by Benjamin Warner, about 1870. H. 1 ft. 5 in. W. 1 ft. 9 in.   T.94a–1930

7. Wallpaper frieze designed by Bruce J. Talbert (1838–81). Made by Jeffrey and Co., 1877. H. 2 ft. 2 in. W. 1 ft. 9½ in.   E.1855–1934

8. Decanter, silver mounted glass bottle set with precious stones and antique coins. Designed by William Burges (1827–81) and made by Richard A. Green, 1866. H. 11 in. W. 7 in.   Circ. 857–1956

9. Teapot, e.p.n.s. with ebony handle. Designed by Christopher Dresser (1834–1904) about 1880, and made by James Dixon and Sons, Sheffield. H. 4⅓ in. L. 9¾ in. W. 4¾ in. In the possession of the makers.

10. Oak table. Designed by Philip Webb (1831–1915), about 1870. H. 2 ft. 5 in. L. 5 ft. 5 in. W. 1 ft. 11½ in.   W.45–1926

11. Wardrobe, painted and gilt. Probably designed by Philip Webb. The door painted by Sir Edward Burne-Jones (1833–98) with subjects from 'The Prioress's Tale' and with flowers on the sides painted by William Morris (1834–96); 1858. H. 4 ft. 3 in. W. 4 ft. 1 in. D. 1 ft. 4 in. On loan from the Ashmolean Museum, Oxford.

12. Wallpaper, 'Pimpernel', designed by William Morris and made by Jeffrey and Co.; 1876. H. 2 ft. 5 in. W. 1 ft. 10½ in.   E.497–1919

13. Printed cotton, 'Tulip and Willow', designed by William Morris about 1873 and printed by Morris and Co., at Merton Abbey about 1889. H. 3 ft. W. 2 ft. 6 in.   Circ. 89–1933

14. Tapestry panel, 'Flora'. The figure designed by Sir Edward Burne-Jones, the background by William Morris. Woven by Morrris and Co., at Merton Abbey, 1885. H. 10 ft. W. 7 ft. 5 in. In the possession of the Whitworth Art Gallery, Manchester.

15. Pottery designed by William De Morgan (1839–1917).
Covered vase, lustre-painted. Made at Fulham, 1888–98. H. 11¾ in. Diam. 8⅞ in.   C.413–1919
Dish, lustre painted, probably at Merton Abbey, 1882-88. Diam. 14½ in.
                                        632–1905
Vase, painted in 'Persian' colours. Made at Merton Abbey, 1887 or earlier. H. 12¾ in. Diam. 11⅜ in.   407–1887

16. Late Victorian and Edwardian Pottery.
Vase, parian porcelain, decorated in 'pâte-sur-pâte' by M. L. Solon for Mintons, 1873. H. 10¼ in. L. 8 in. W. 4¼ in.   573a–1877
Covered jar, painted in lustre by Richard Joyce for Pilkingtons, about 1909. H. 4⅞ in. Diam. 5 in. In the possession of the Manchester City Art Galleries.
Vase, with sgraffito decoration by Charles Collis and painted by Liza Wilkins at the Della Robbia Pottery, Birkenhead, 1899. H. 15¼ in. Diam. 5¾ in. In the possession of the Williamson Art Gallery, Birkenhead.
Jug, saltglaze stoneware, decorated, by George Tinworth for Doultons, Lambeth, 1872. H. 9½ in. Diam. 5⅝ in.   348–1874

17. Tankard. Saltglazed stoneware designed and made by the Martin Brothers. Made by R. Wallace Martin at Fulham, about 1874. H. $8\frac{1}{8}$ in. Diam. $4\frac{1}{4}$ in.   3769-1901

Vase. Made at Southhall, 1886. H. $8\frac{1}{2}$ in. Diam. $5\frac{1}{2}$ in.   C.1154-1917

Jug. Made at Southall, 1900. H. $8\frac{3}{8}$ in. Diam. $6\frac{3}{4}$ in.   C.493-1919

Vase. Made at Southall, 1903. H. 10 in. Diam. $7\frac{1}{2}$ in.   C.468-1919

18. Furniture designed by E. W. Godwin (1838–86).

Coffee table, painted or ebonized oak. Made by William Watt, 1867. H. 2 ft. 3 in. W. 1 ft. 4 in. On loan from the City Art Gallery, Bristol.

Chair, oak. Made by William Watt, about 1880. H. 3 ft. 6 in. W. 3 ft. 2 in.   Circ. 258-1958

19. 'Cromer Bird'. Printed cotton designed by A. H. Mackmurdo (1851–1942). Printed by Simpson and Godlee, Manchester, for the Century Guild, about 1884. H. 3 ft. W. 2 ft. 9 in.   T.88-1953

20. Nursery wallpaper, 'The Sleeping Beauty' designed by Walter Crane (1845–1915). Made by Jeffrey and Co., about 1875. H. 2 ft. 6 in. W. 1 ft. 10 in.   Circ. 566-1931

21. Machine-printed cotton designed by Lewis F. Day (1845–1910). Made by Turnbull and Stockdale, 1898. H. 2 ft. 5 in. W. 2 ft.   T.17-1954

22. 'Purple Bird'. Woven fabric, silk and wool, designed by C. F. A. Voysey (1857–1941) and made by Alexander Morton and Co., 1899. H. 2 ft. 5 in. W. 1 ft. $10\frac{1}{2}$ in.   T.20-1953

23. Group of furniture designed by C. F. A. Voysey.

Oak desk, with brass hinge made by W. H. Tingey, 1896. H. 5 ft. 6 in. W. 2 ft. 9 in. D. 2 ft. 10 in.   W.6-1953

Oak chair made by Story and Co., 1899. H. 4 ft. 4 in. W. 1 ft. 5 in. Lent by Mrs. J. Bottard.

'Green Pastures'. Machine-woven Axminster carpet, made by Tomkinson and Adam, Kidderminster, 1896. W. 3 ft. 9 in. L. 4 ft. 7 in.   T.72-1953

24. Chair and table, oak, designed by Charles Rennie Mackintosh (1868–1928) for the Glasgow School of Art, 1897. Chair, H. 4 ft, $6\frac{1}{2}$ in. W. 1 ft. 7 in. Table, H. 2 ft. $6\frac{1}{2}$ in. W. 2 ft. 2 in. In the possession of the School of Art.

25. Cushion cover, linen appliqué on linen embroidered with coloured silks. Designed and worked by Jessie Newbery (b. 1864), about 1900. H. 1 ft. $10\frac{1}{2}$ in. W. 2 ft. $1\frac{1}{2}$ in.   T.69-1953

Mirror frame, 'Honesty', in pure tin. Designed and made by Margaret and Frances Macdonald, 1896. H. 2 ft. 5 in. W. 2 ft. 4 in. In the possession of the Glasgow Art Gallery.

26. Hall table, birchwood, inlaid with ebony, 1908. H. 2 ft. 4 in. L. 3 ft. D. 1 ft. 4 in., and candlestick, steel, 1888. H. 1 ft. 6 in. Designed by George Walton (1867–1933). Candlestick Circ. 124-1959; table in the possession of Sir Ronald Davison.

27. Bed curtain, appliqué of silk on felt, embroidered in coloured silks.

Designed by M. H. Baillie-Scott (1865–1945). H. 2 ft. 11½ in. W. 1 ft. 3½ in. In the possession of Mrs. Lister Wallis.

Child's chair, oak with inlaid decoration and leather seat. Designed by M. H. Baillie-Scott and made by J. P. White, Bedford, about 1901. H. 3 ft. 4¼ in. W. 1 ft. 9½ in. In the possession of Sir Andrew MacTaggart.

28. Late Victorian and Edwardian Glass.

Cameo vase, decorated by C. Northwood for Stevens & Williams, 1884. H. 8¼ in. Diam. 4⅜ in. In the possession of the makers.

Vase, made by James Powell & Sons; about 1900. H. 8¾ in. Diam. 4⅝ in. In the possession of P. G. Ledster, Esq.

Decanter, decorated by William Fritsche at Thomas Webb & Sons; probably during the 1890's. H. 13⅝ in. Diam. 4¾ in. In the possession of the makers.

Vase, with trailed decoration. Made by A. Stanier for Stuart & Sons; about 1905. H. 15¼ in. Diam. 4⅛ in. In the possession of the makers.

29. Late Victorian and Edwardian Jewellery.

Peacock brooch, gold, silver, chased and set with mother-of-pearl. Designed by C. R. Ashbee (1863–1942) and executed by the Guild of Handicrafts, about 1900. H. 5 in. W. 2⅜ in. In the possession of Miss Jean Stewart.

Pendant and buckle, silver with gold detail decorated with enamelling and set with semi-precious stones. Designed and executed by Henry Wilson (1864–1934), about 1905. Pendant, H. 6 in. Buckle, W. 7 in. Lent by Miss Enid Morse.

Pendant, silver decorated with enamelling and set with semi-precious stones and pearls. Designed and executed by Arthur Gaskin (1862–1929), 1906. H. 3½ in. In the possession of Mrs. J. V. Charlewood-Turner.

30. Teapot, electro-plate on brass with a cane handle. Designed by W. A. S. Benson (1854–1924) and executed by W. A. S. Benson and Co., about 1900. H. 5 in. Diam. 6½ in. In the possession of Capt. and Mrs Michael Sumner.

Chafing dish, silver, hand raised with stamped and cast details. Designed by Henry Wilson; about 1906. H. 9¾ in. Diam. 11 in. In the possession of the Worshipful Company of Goldsmiths.

31. Child's oak chair inlaid with ebony, mother-of pearl and ivory. Designed by Ambrose Heal (b. 1872) and made by Heal and Son, 1901. H. 6 ft. 3 in. W. 3 ft. 9 in. D. 1 ft. 1 in. In the possession of Moray Angus, Esq.

32. Cabinet on stand, ebony inlaid with mother-of-pearl. Designed by Ernest Gimson (1864–1920), about 1910. H. 3 ft. 10½ in. W. 2 ft. 3 in. D. 1 ft. 2 in. In the possession of the City of Leicester Museum and Art Gallery.